W9-ADL-337

MAY 2 2011

GREAT WARRIORS

KNIGHTS

KATE RIGGS

CREATIVE 🍎 EDUCATION

Published by Creative Education
P.O. Box 227, Mankato, Minnesota 56002
Creative Education is an imprint of The Creative Company
www.thecreativecompany.us

Design and production by Stephanie Blumenthal
Art direction by Rita Marshall
Printed by Corporate Graphics in the United States of America

Photographs by Alamy (The Art Gallery Collection, Mary Evans Picture Library, North Wind Picture Archives,
Popperfoto), Corbis (Bettmann, Ramon Manent, Museum of M.D. Mallorca, Baldwin H. Ward &
Kathryn C. Ward), Getty Images (Bridgeman Art Library, Hulton Archive), iStockphoto

Library of Congress Cataloging-in-Publication Data
Riggs, Kate.
Knights / by Kate Riggs.
p. cm. — (Great warriors)
Summary: A simple introduction to the European warriors known as knights, including their history, lifestyle,
weapons, and how they remain a part of today's culture through books and films.
Includes index.
ISBN 978-1-60818-001-1
1. Knights and knighthood—Europe—History—Juvenile literature. 2. Civilization, Medieval—Juvenile
literature. I. Title. II. Series.
CR4513.R54 2011
940.1—dc22   2009048805
CPSIA: 040110 PO1137
First Edition
2 4 6 8 9 7 5 3 1

TABLE OF CONTENTS

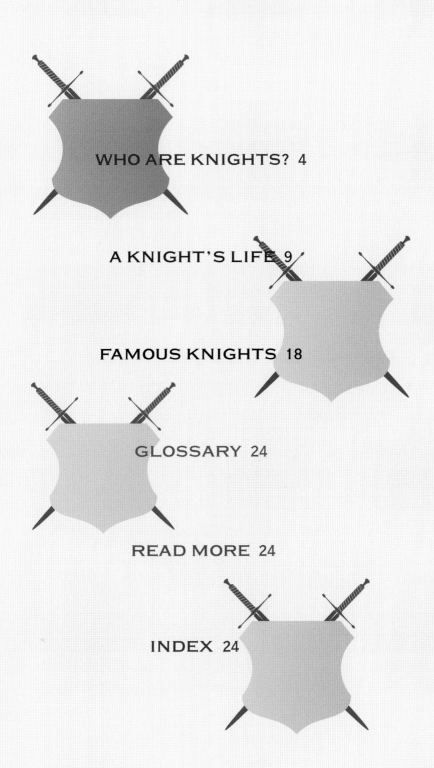

WHO ARE KNIGHTS? 4

A KNIGHT'S LIFE 9

FAMOUS KNIGHTS 18

GLOSSARY 24

READ MORE 24

INDEX 24

Sometimes people fight.

They fight for food. They fight for land.

Or sometimes they fight for sport.

Knights were warriors who fought other

people to protect their **lord** and his land.

Knights often had a very dangerous job

Knights first fought in Europe (*YOO-rup*) about 1,500 years ago. They lived during the **Middle Ages**. At that time, lords and kings owned most of the land. Knights were soldiers who were paid to fight for a lord or king.

A king's knights (bottom) protected his castle (top)

WHEN KNIGHTS SURROUNDED A CASTLE OR TOWN, IT WAS
CALLED LAYING SIEGE (*SEEJ*) TO IT.

Boys started training to be knights when they were young. They learned how to read and write. They learned about weapons. Then they watched older knights and learned from them.

Boys helped older knights get ready for battle

A knight carried many weapons into battle. He had a long, sharp sword. He also used a shorter knife. Most knights used long, heavy sticks called lances. A lance had a sharp point at the end.

Knights had their weapons with them all the time

SOME KNIGHTS USED A MACE. THIS WAS A POLE WITH A HEAVY METAL BALL AT THE END.

Some knights rode horses when they fought. Others walked. But all knights wore a suit of **armor**. The armor was made out of strong metal like iron and steel.

Tiny hoops of metal were linked together in chain mail

SOME KNIGHTS WORE ARMOR CALLED CHAIN MAIL. IT WAS LIKE METAL CLOTHING.

Knights fought on battlefields. Two armies of knights charged toward each other and fought until one side gave up. Then the army that won took over the land.

An army was a large group of knights who fought together

ARCHERS SOMETIMES HELPED KNIGHTS IN BATTLE. THEY SHOT ARROWS AT THE OTHER ARMY.

Knights lived by a set of rules called chivalry (*SHIV-ul-ree*). Chivalry taught knights to be kind and brave. When knights were not fighting, they took care of their own land. Most knights married and had children.

A knight's land was sometimes near a king's castle

Many knights became heroes. Edward the Black Prince was a knight who lived in England. He was the son of a king. Another famous knight was a king. Richard the Lionhearted fought in wars called the **Crusades.**

St. George (top) was famous for killing a dragon

THERE ARE STILL KNIGHTS TODAY. BUT THEY DO NOT FIGHT. "KNIGHT" IS JUST A NAME OF HONOR.

By the 1500s, knights stopped fighting as much. Countries used bigger armies instead. But knights are still popular in movies and stories. Today, some people even like to dress up as knights. They relive the times of the great knights!

A queen or king names a person as a knight

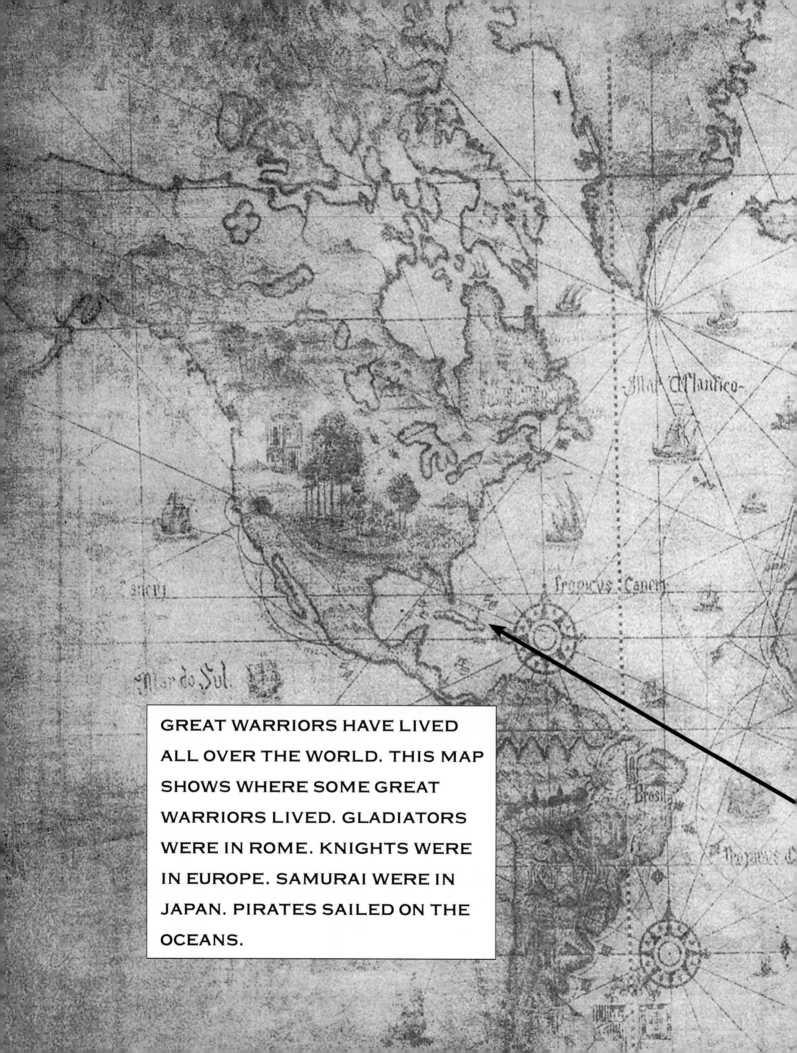

GREAT WARRIORS HAVE LIVED ALL OVER THE WORLD. THIS MAP SHOWS WHERE SOME GREAT WARRIORS LIVED. GLADIATORS WERE IN ROME. KNIGHTS WERE IN EUROPE. SAMURAI WERE IN JAPAN. PIRATES SAILED ON THE OCEANS.

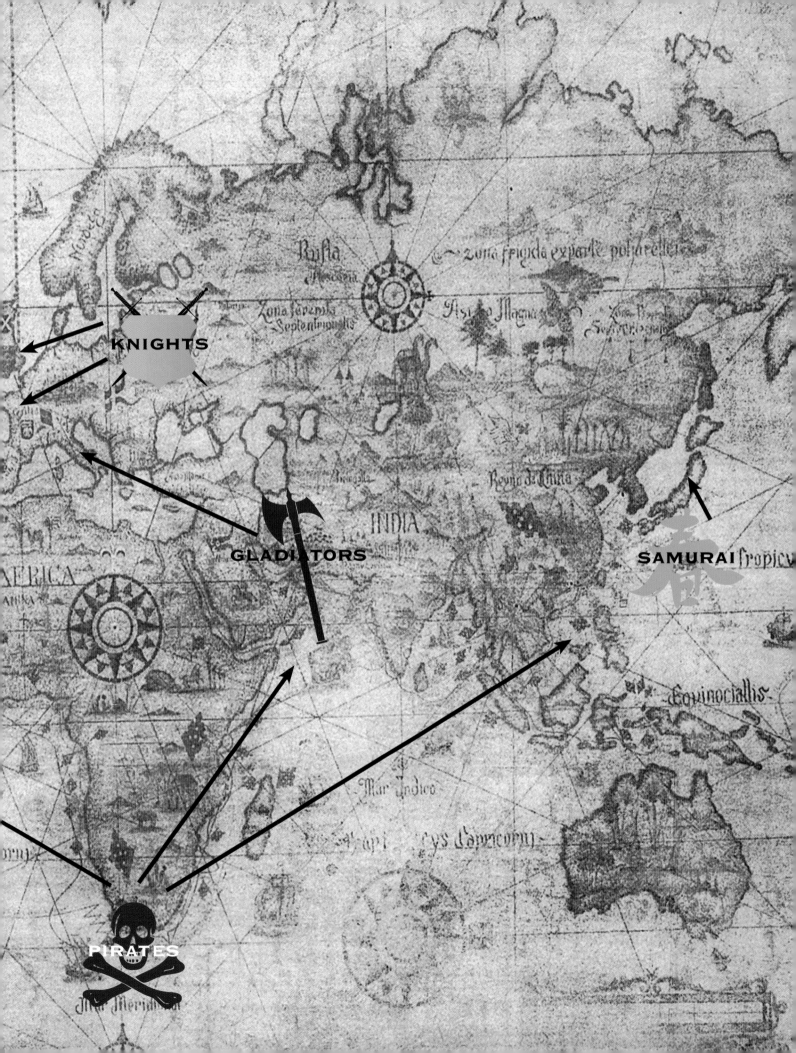

GLOSSARY

archers—people who shoot bows and arrows

armor—metal coverings that knights wore to protect their bodies in battle

Crusades—wars fought between A.D. 1095 and 1291 by people from Europe against people in the Holy Land (where the countries of Israel and Palestine are today)

lord—a rich man in charge of all the people who lived on his land

Middle Ages—the time period from A.D. 476 to 1453

READ MORE

Gigliotti, Jim. *Knight Life*. Mankato, Minn.: Child's World, 2009.

Steele, Philip. *Navigators: Knights & Castles*. New York: Kingfisher, 2008.

INDEX

armies 14, 15, 21

armor 12, 13

battles 10, 14, 15

chivalry 17

Edward the Black Prince 18

Europe 6, 18

horses 12

kings 6, 18

lifestyle 17

lords 4, 6

Middle Ages 6

training 9

weapons 9, 10, 11